A Brief History of Time

SHAINDEL BEERS' poetry, fiction, and creative nonfiction have appeared in numerous journals and anthologies. She is currently an instructor of English at Blue Mountain Community College in the Eastern Oregon high desert town of Pendleton, and serves as Poetry Editor of *Contrary* (www.contrarymagazine.com). She hosts the talk radio poetry show Translated By, which can be found at http://www.blogtalkradio.com/onword.

A Brief History of Time

Shaindel Beers

SALT

CAMBRIDGE

PUBLISHED BY SALT PUBLISHING
14a High Street, Fulbourn, Cambridge CB21 5DH United Kingdom

First published 2009

Printed and bound in the United States by Lightning Source Inc

Typeset in Swift 9.5 / 13

ISBN 978 1 84471 505 3 paperback

Salt Publishing Ltd gratefully acknowledges
the financial assistance of Arts Council England

1 3 5 7 9 8 6 4 2

For all of my teachers, and for Lee,
who teaches me every day.

Contents

Acknowledgments

Grateful acknowledgment is made to the journals and anthologies in which these poems, some of them in earlier versions, first appeared:

Poetry Miscellany: "A Brief History of Time"; *A Prairie Home Companion* (website): "First Love"; *Women. Period.*: "Elegy for a Past Life"; *Eight Octaves Review*: "Stretching out that fifteen minutes"; *Thieves Jargon*: "Triptych—The Light, The End, The Light" and "Why Gold-digging Fails"; *the minnesota review*: "HA!" and "The Thermophobic's Wife"; *hotmetalpress.net*, *Dust* (reprint), and *Open Windows III* (reprint): "Sleeping Man and Woman, Circa 2000, C.E."; *The New Verse News*: "For Stephen Funk, in Prison for Protesting the Iraq War"; *Tipton Poetry Journal*: "Sunday Worship"; *The DuPage Review*: "Fitriani *in front of her house*"; *Red Fez*: "Last Train from the City"; *Hunger Mountain*: "Why It Almost Never Ends with Stripping"; *The Guild of Outsider Writers* (website): "To CKC, Stillborn, April 22, 2006"; Talkin' Blues: "Rewind"; *Aftershocks: The Poetry of Recovery for Life-Shattering Events*: "A Study in Weights and Measures"; *Alternatives to Surrender*: "Surgery"; *I Am This Meat*: "Body Shop"; *Eleventh Muse*: "What Will We Do With You? This Bone Has Almost No Flesh Protecting It—"; *The Apple Valley Review*: "My Love, A Partial Explanation" and "Belonging"; *The Poetry of Relationships*: "Taking Back the Bra Drawer"; *Trellis Magazine*: "Moonlight Sestina".

My thanks to both Blue Mountain Community College and Seminole Community College, for financing my trips to writers' conferences and workshops to further this work. Thanks, especially, to Vermont College of the Fine Arts and my terrific advisors there—Natasha Sajé, Clare Rossini, Richard Jackson, and Leslie Ullman. Thanks, also, to my VCFA workshop leaders and discriminating workshop members, as well as to Charles Harper Webb, my post-graduate manuscript advisor. Gratitude to the teachers who believed in me, Kenneth Deal and Claire Clements, especially, from Huntingdon College; and Nancy Miller and Jan Chittum, even before that. My parents, for a love of books, regardless of what little else we had. It is what has helped me navigate the world. To my students who teach me far more than I teach them. To Michael Beaudoin, for his keen proofreading. Love to the Salt family—Chris and Jen Hamilton-Emery—the type of publishers every writer dreams of having. And to my husband—Thank you for *being*.

A Brief History of Time

Now that we each have someone who knows how
we take our coffee, that smallest but most telling of intimacies—
you, black, three sweeteners; me, cream, no sugar—
we're each eating breakfast with other people who don't
drink coffee at all. There seems to be a message here, but
I don't know what it is. I'm no good at this love thing

nonetheless, I keep on trying, like the benchwarmer
who begs to be sent in and is carried out crushed every time.
I wish just once someone would
cry out from the stands, *Quit putting her in there.*
For God's sake, she's just a kid. She'll get killed
if she takes much more. Then I could go back
to my regular duties of pouring Gatorade,
wiping away sweat and shards of bicuspids and
incisors. But this never happens. The Elizabethans were right,
you know, that love is just another type of insanity. The Greeks
thought the seat of love was the eyes;
the liver, the seat of desire;
and the Tongans of Australia believe it resides
in manava *'o fafine 'a e nofo'anga 'o e 'ofa*, the womb of a woman.

I'm sure it's an electrical impulse that travels
our most twisted neurons, axons, and dendrites—or
why would we fall into the trap of doing the same thing
the same way and expect different results, which is
one definition of insanity? This would explain why my father is
still married to my mother, even after she tried to knife him
just days after coming home from jail
for two other attempted murders.

This definition was
put forth by one Gerald Nadler (Ph.D.), President of the Center
for Breakthrough Thinking, the people who write those books
about how to be a "team player" and your "best self"

for the purpose of making other people rich. When I tried
my hand at financial planning, I did it to help people, probably
another symptom of my psychosis, wanting my neighbors
to be able to send their kids to college, and when other planners asked
what I did the rest of the time, I said *write poetry*,
and they asked me to write about our company, which wasn't
at all poetic.

So I left. But not without a huge life
insurance policy and annuities, so that if marriage is
a war of attrition, the survivor will come out loaded—and to me,
this doesn't seem cynical because I think we've both
earned our field pay these past six years. And it makes us better
off than the *bushi*, who were paid in rice and had to barter the rest,
but not as good as the *hatamoto*, who received fiefs from their *daimayo*.
Because after all, isn't one's own space the best refuge?
At least, according to Virginia Woolf, who couldn't get enough
of her own life, and chose to end it.

I think I'm through with being in love with people
though I'll love mountains as only a flatlander can. To be awed
by something so big and unyielding that your desire
to conquer it never dies, though you know in your heart,
liver, neurons, axons, dendrites, and womb, that it will
never happen. Because the Rockies, my latest non-human love,
were born 65 million years ago, maybe the same year a meteor crashed
near the Yucatan, rendering the dinosaurs irrelevant
except to squirmy kindergarteners who love them
and to paleontologist Paul Sereno, who was named one of *People*
      magazine's
"50 Most Beautiful People" which, unfortunately, is
probably how most people know him, not as discoverer
of *Deltadromeus agilis*, (Agile River Runner) and
Eoraptor lunensis (Dawn Plunderer), although this isn't entirely true
because these were discovered by members of his expedition team

but have the most lovely names, so I've decided to change
history, by writing these untruths, the way
Lydia Howard Sigourney rewrote an entire culture in 1841
with her *Pocahontas and Other Poems*, following
James Fenimore Cooper's lead of exchanging Mohegans
for Mohicans and claiming in his novel that they'd become extinct,
which perhaps has caused teenagers in the Hudson River Valley
and Uncasville, Connecticut to wonder if they really exist at all,
the way I used to wonder if I really existed
when I sat with Jenny on the hood of her 1983 Cutlass Supreme
on nights when the moon was full and we'd talk about how
it looked like a good night to die.
That same moon I liked to picture as a baseball, years earlier,
a baseball hit so hard and far that nothing could ever bring it back.

Would you know me

if you had met me in my natural environs
wearing the uniform
of the hardworking rural poor—
straight-legged jeans, plaid flannel,
ponytail pulled through the back
of a John Deere cap,
a nondescript girl with hair as dun as after-harvest fields,
eyes the color of a Midwestern sky
that doesn't
even make it
to blue
nine months of the year,
a bleak heart to match the landscape
of that land where winter never ends—

there's a chance you would have stopped
in August
at the roadside stand
where I used to sell the extra produce
my family could never use by season's end—
sweet corn, twelve ears for a dollar,
tomatoes, still warm from the sun—
you would have named your price and maybe wondered

about that quiet girl
who deftly filled your bags,
her small hands,
fingers flat and broad from honest work,
but you never would have thought
of all that she had done for your
dollar ninety-five—
hefting hay to feed the calves
and shoveling mounds of warm
manure to fertilize the soil months before
those tomatoes and corn

[4]

were pushed into the earth,
dropping fat green tomato bugs into coffee cans
of gasoline, pulling weeds in ninety-degree
sun so the ears would grow full
and yellow and ripe

so you could take them away
and forget me
until you meet me years later
in my favorite disguise—sophisticated city-dweller
where I am cast under silver lunar streams
in a platinum glow, no longer
grey and dun,
a new creature,
and you could proclaim it destiny.

First Love

Anxious for the nine o'clock break,
at eight-thirty I would light the porch,
line the sink with gauze, cotton balls, peroxide—
austere tools of love—
wanting him to bring his hands to me—
small, delicate hands
an artist's or surgeon's
displaced by the lack of a diploma,
twisting wires ten hours a day.

When his Grand Prix rumbled into the drive,
I would look not at his face
but his hands
and nightly make the same, sharp sigh
when I had counted *ten*
like a new mother,
knowing that metal which cuts bricks
could lay siege to fingers too.

I'd fold his hands in mine
like folding sugar into butter
and lead him past my disapproving parents
to my makeshift triage
under the fluorescent buzz of bathroom lights.
Awed by the horrid beauty
of miniscule rivulets of blood,
the muted glitter of metal shards
just under the skin,

I'd begin my gentle ritual
of tweezing out steel slivers,
flooding the red rivers white with peroxide,
softly blowing away the sting—
then, I would send him back, bandaged,

with a sandwich,
to the big, block building just outside of town
and return to my geometry.

Elegy for a Past Life

I miss the honest life we used to lead
scraping up odd jobs so we could see
a movie the next town over,
and stare for a few hours at people
on the drive-in screen who weren't
like us—who didn't wear too big hand-me-down
flannels and mud-caked boots—
and even if they were playing farm people,
had never known that pinching pain
in the sacral spine that paralyzes
as you heft the bale by the twine
and let it avalanche down to the ground.

For days, after seeing a show, we'd sit in the loft,
legs dangling over the bleating sheep below
and dream about the life we'd live
when we'd escaped. Back then at sixteen
I thought we'd make it out together,
and become writers, the only job we could imagine
where we wouldn't smell like shit or hay or cows

but too many months passed when I didn't bleed
and when we were safe, the test negative
and burned in the rubbish heap behind the barn,
you left, too afraid of being trapped
in a cornfield town
to wait for me.

Red Heifer

There was the year of all-black cattle,
except for the small, red heifer
I wanted to be mine

from the second she ambled down the ramp
of the livestock truck
just because she was different
and a "she."

I begged to be taught to milk her,
counted days until she'd be old enough,
asked if I could spend the night
in a sleeping bag

out in the barn
waiting for her to give birth
the way that I'd seen grown-ups do.

Names of other cattle have stayed with me
Floyd, whose name was later prefaced
by *Fat*, and *Maynard*, who,
weighing in at 2,000 lbs
would still come when you whistled

but I can't for anything
remember the name of that red heifer,

just that she took away my pain
when Grandpa yanked my Band-Aid off,
pointing to her across the field
as a distraction.

Stretching out that fifteen minutes

Exploding flashes of cameras. Crackle of microphones magnifying wind. So much attention. Dizzying. Unreal. Excited yips of dogs picking up the scent. Beating down rows and rows of corn. Looks like a TV special on crop circles. Shouts, sometimes carried far on prairie breeze, *Kohhhhh-Deeee*, sometimes choked down throats in the rasping wind, Koh-dee. Internal film reel replaying pleas on Channel 22 News—*Please help me find my son . . . I just want Cody back. If you've seen him . . .* Pull picture out of purse. Look imploringly at Camera One. Sheriff warns of gopher traps set in fields, pack of wild dogs spotted on Johnson's farm down the road. *Not trying to scare you, Ma'am. Just want you to be prepared. Just in case.* Neighbors bring over dinner *so you won't have to cook, more important things to worry about, but you still need to eat.* So much food—peach cobbler, beef and noodles, a whole ham, peanut butter pie—so nice of them. Watch for his face on the nine o'clock news. Wonder how many hearts are breaking—*that poor woman. Darling little boy, only six years old.* How many gruff men saying, *Damn kids shouldn't play in cornfields, 'course you'll get lost—nothing but corn for miles. And they crush the corn.* Next morning, sunup, search resumes. Everyone soaked in dew, chipper, hopeful, volunteers handing out free Dunkin' Donuts coffee. Feature local story on the early news at five—weary farmers watch for trading price of grain, soybeans, hogs, over morning coffee. Bewildered cry of a hound, excited shouts, *Over here! We found him!* Large man has swooped him up. *He was just here, huddling between the rows.* Sheriff brings mylar blanket. *He's cold, but he'll be fine!*, he announces. Crowd cheers. Your few minutes of fame are up—next time, you'll have to hide him better.

Triptych—The Light, The End, The Light

The lawn is a coarse, green carpet
waiting to shred my feet
so my oxygenless blood can feed its roots.
Heavy clouds suffocate my cries.
It has picked a perfect day to drown me.
I slide into the soil.
The metallic taste of dirt fills me—
nose, mouth, and lungs. Days pass.
A sharp stab of light wakes me
when a shovel breaks ground, just missing
my head. It is little Jimmy Millican,
from next door, attempting, again,
to dig to China. He has heard the women there
are beautiful, and he misses his mother.
No, he doesn't miss her, but the *idea*
of her, a different idea entirely
than the one his father has, every night,
sitting in his boxers on the edge
of the narrow bed, downing another oxycontin
to bring on sleep. "Dad!" screams Jimmy—
"A girl is buried in the yard!"
"Stop fucking around Jimmy—It's not
funny! That astounding sound of loneliness
when the first shovelful of dirt
hit your mother's coffin—" but he trails off,
train of thought lost in a cloud of numbness.
Jimmy reaches down, pulls me out—
his father's gone again. He has to be the man now.
"You better watch it, Blondie," his father mutters,
"Next time, Jimmy here might not be digging
for worms." An orange glower from Jimmy
aimed at Dad—"I will so be digging—Now I know
we have a pretty lady patch in the front yard."
"Qué loco—" his father nods knowingly.
We all worry for Jimmy but not enough

because in ten years he will think the electric fence
is talking to him—asking him to feed it things—
At first turtles and frogs,
then kittens. Until one day, he walks naked
into its embrace—finding the light
a shovel makes when it splits the soil.

A Man Walks Into a Bar

He was tall, well-built, blue-eyed,
a guy most girls would want to take to bed.
Then he reached for the beer with his left hand,
revealing the stump of his right.

We could tell the second he knew that we knew.
We'd smile, but the smile wouldn't travel
all the way to our eyes. He'd turn back to the bar,
fold his arm closer so that we could
no longer see

as we rushed off to sling beers for guys
not as good-looking but more whole,
the ones who leered lecherously,
on "Short-Shorts Night"
and left ten dollar tips for two dollar beers

always expecting more, always bitter when we didn't deliver.
The quiet one, we wounded week after week, a guy
any of us would have considered "out of our league,"
"a long shot," if he had been unbroken,

the sad, blond man we were afraid to love.

Why Gold-digging Fails

I.

Because there was the tattoo artist
who took us for rides on his motorcycle
and gave Jenny the hand-sized fairy on her stomach
that she swore she'd never ruin by getting pregnant

and the most beautiful guy we'd ever seen
who was cruising with his friend in an olive green
hooptie that we hoped was a sign of his rebellion
against rich parents who maybe had bought him a Mercedes
which he traded for something "more sensible"
because something about him seemed rich
and not at all small-town, and we didn't know
who he was, until on a break from college

I was out with a friend who said, "I should stop by
and see my friend Mike. Want to meet him?"
We waited in a dark living room decorated in
early nineties thrift store—dank green sofas,
padding pluming out the cushions—talking
to a doughy blonde girl who must have been pretty
thirty pounds ago, as she pushed a fat, laughing baby
in one of those yellow and white gingham swings
that clickety-clacks as they unwind,
when in walked the guy we'd always wanted,
not dressed down for a rich guy but dressed up
for one of us—
neatly pressed flannel tucked into Wranglers
nearly hiding tawny construction boots,
like the ones I wore when roofing—
and there was that odd moment of recognition
and fumbling for words
when quantum theory hit me and I realized
if we'd tried harder instead of merely flirting

in parking lots at the beach and the Dairy Queen
and the drive-in that sold gallons of homemade root beer
either of us could be that chubby blonde woman
with the fat baby
and the happy husband waiting for green olive burgers
in our own little utopia
ten miles further than our mothers got.

II.

Because every time we hung out at the billiards room
of the Condos at the lake,
the rich people gave us dirty looks.
They knew what we were up to—
two blonde girls in Daisy Dukes
and bikini tops
in a borrowed sports car
hunting for rich boyfriends,
anything to get us out of Argos, Indiana.
My grandmother, also, must have tried this bit,
working as a dishwasher in the kitchen
of the academy. My brother, too, worked there.
Maybe his motives were more pure.
All I know is for Jenny and me none of this worked.
Her one rich boyfriend used to beat her
to a pulp; and I decided to leave my marriage
with enough money to fix a timing belt,
just in case my engine decided to go.
Our parents had tried to warn us. They knew our game.
The rich aren't like you and me, my father used to say,
The rich aren't like you and me.

"HA!"

There's so much wrong with a country where a woman
dying of ovarian cancer has to work forty hours a week
at Dollar General; and with the stock boy, who when he
finds out why she is in the bathroom all the time,
starts to call her "HA!" behind her back, which stands
for "Hemorrhaging Ann," and he thinks it is hilarious.
This, of course, is hilarious, because everything is
fucking hilarious when you're nineteen and working
a good-for-shit job where you can keep your hash pipe
in a baggie in the dumpster behind the store
and volunteer to take out trash six nights a week
and get paid to get stoned off your ass.
And I think things can't get worse for Ann
until the night when the cashier
who I've always thought was beautiful
in that over-fucked-underfed way that addicts have
comes in after she's been fired
(for shooting up in her car when she claimed
she was calling home to check on her little girl)
to pick up her last paycheck and grabs a package
of tighty whities (a 3-pack for $5)
and rips it open and puts a pair on Ann's head
and leaves the store, laughing, with her paycheck.
And I wish there was something I could do—
give Ann money, which I don't have,
so she could take her kids somewhere nice
and let them know their mom for the last
six months, three months, whatever
she's got left; or find her a real job somewhere
where she doesn't have to work with junkies
and get yelled at by people who don't understand
that if the sign says "3 for $1," you have to buy 3
because it's "Dollar General" and all the prices
are even, but I can't even get myself a job
that I'd want to work now, let alone if I had only

three months left. But perhaps karma
will take care of it somehow, like when the
one nice cashier, who Ann thinks is a slut
and doesn't know defended her,
tells the stock boy, "Steve, don't think that couldn't happen
to your girlfriend someday,"
and not a week later, she has a miscarriage,
and he has to drive her to the hospital
where she loses more blood than Ann has in a month.

The Thermophobic's Wife

Twenty years in the steel mill, and now he can't
keep cool enough. She does everything she can—
has a cold shower running at the first crunch of gravel,
lets him sleep naked on top of white eyelet sheets
under the fan, the thermostat turned down to fifty.
When they make love she takes a stainless steel bowl
from the pot and pan cabinet, sets it on the nightstand,
full of ice, takes the slippery cubes between her lips,
her fingers. They become a part of her as she tends to him.
She is a nurse, a wife, of ice.

She has wanted to take him on a vacation to see Hank's grave,
and now that he has spent his life in *hot as hell*
five days a week since age nineteen, he won't go south
of Indianapolis for anything—daughters' weddings, nephews'
funerals. She can't convince him that these places are not hot
all year round. He's a take-no-chances kind of man.
His need for cold means she will tend runt piglets
under the heat lamp in the kitchen,
yellow chicks in incubators;
she is the caretaker of greenhouse
tomatoes, the sage and rosemary that soak up the meager
Midwestern sun while he toils in red hot, white hot.
She has built her life around the cold—
the grey blue house, the white trim, the dark wood—
her life has been winter as long as she can remember,
and she prays that it is a long time,
a cold day in hell or heaven
or the north woods of Wisconsin, wherever he will go
when he is gone.

Sleep

They would scrawl their hate on my message board
nightly after you left—*bitch, slut, cunt, whore,*
never bothering to ask me the truth,
more fun to make up rumors of uncouth
acts behind closed doors. *Why else would he slink
to her, all hours of the night?* Who would think
without knowing your story of a lost
little boy, no parents—days of exhaustion
eighteen years later, afraid to sleep
alone, so sure history would repeat
itself. I'd hold you close, *shhhshhh* to keep
you quiet and feel eerily complete
with you, sound asleep, cradled on my chest.
Of all the gifts I've given, giving you sleep
was best.

Sleeping Man and Woman, Circa 2000, C.E.

Under the glass, they lie curled
like rosebuds against themselves;
her head is on his chest
perennially listening for a heartbeat
which will not come. His lips retain
the slightest curve of a smile;
his arm encircles her.
They seem to have simply fallen asleep
forever.
        Spectators travel from around the world
to see this couple—to witness the wonder that was
centuries ago: the clothing, so odd;
the ungainliness of the bodies;
the awkward cut of the hair. So this
was what life was like? It remains a mystery
what froze them like this.
        No volcanic ash
like Pompeii to enshroud them,
no ice to preserve their still pink flesh
like that of the mammoths in Siberia—
It is not clear where they came from.
The curator does not remember
because the curator before him
does not remember—

It is as if they just appeared, here,
in the museum, out of a fairy tale,
waiting to be awakened. And that is
the irrevocable feeling. That is why
the visitors slow their breathing
when they enter the vault,
why the only sound is a quick intake of breath
from each passerby
at the astounding silence.

No one is tempted to wake them
because there have been ninety-seven wars,
twenty-five earthquakes,
three billion five hundred fifty thousand and seventy-nine
tears shed since they relinquished consciousness;

that is why the awe, the confusion
at this display of peace.

For Stephen Funk, in Prison for Protesting the Iraq War

Stephen-in-your-cell, would you forgive me
if from now on, I promise to be brave?
When I picture you alone—and lonely
I wonder how I could have been so weak
to have gone home the first time I was asked.
Protesters should be made of stronger stuff.

Lately things have made me question the stuff
I'm made of. What is it that makes me *me*?
Would I give my life for a cause, if asked?
What is it within us that makes us brave
or, in my case and many others', weak?
And is it true that the strong die lonely

since those who stand for something stand alone?
I wonder what you think of all the stuff
in letters from all of us outside, weak-willed
well-wishers sending thanks, signing meekly
in shaky script, supporting your bravery
from the comfort of our homes. When asked

to protest the war, I failed. One guard asked
me to stop leafleting—so all alone
I put the flyers in my car (such brave
work here) and rewarded myself by stuff-
ing my face with soy burger and fries. My
spirit was lifted—good deed for the week

accomplished. I wasn't faced with my weakness
until the next day when I was asked
about the protest, how it went, and my
stammered answer made me feel so alone
in a world of heroes who've done great stuff
and deserve to live in this "home of the brave."

Stephen, from your story, I've learned bravery.
I've resolved never again to be weak
when it comes to things that matter, the stuff
of life and death. If someday someone asks
you *was it worth it?* know you're not alone
anymore, because you've proven to me

and others that if asked, we can be brave,
that our weakness is not made of different stuff
than courage; it's just us, sure we're not alone.

Sunday Worship

They used to chuckle at him softly
the way the small-minded do at the simpleminded
when he would snore or fart in church—
And sometimes let him carry the collection plate
while they dropped in a sweat-earned buck or two
from callused, earth-caked hands. But it was her I watched—
Imagining how hard it must have been to have
a Mongoloid son and a husband so cruel he called
the boy "It" and left her out of shame. And yet—
she sat there every Sunday of my childhood
beside a forty-something son she still dressed every day
and felt blessed enough with her life
to make me ashamed to pray for more.

Fitriani *in front of her house* . . .

. . . which I would have taken for a chicken coop
if not for the caption

untreated wood as weathered as drift
forms an awning over her head

basket weave of reeds
makes up the wall behind her

she stares stoically *the children have no custom*
of taking pictures for fun

wears a black shirt with red and white flowers
the size of the fists that hang loosely at her sides

she loves mathematics wants to be a teacher
girls often do not finish primary school

black slacks red flip-flops

in the upper corner a green-brown thumbprint—
but whose? Arsad her father *41 never attended school*

works as a peasant farmer grateful
that someone a world away will help his daughter

wearily hands the picture back to Muhtar
community volunteer in Woko Atas

and imagines the hands across the ocean that will hold
the picture of his daughter

will help to pay for uniforms books and pens
wonders if their thumbprints on the picture

will wear away his own

[25]

Last Train from the City

They must have been stoned to move
so slowly
that molecules of still objects
buzzed around them,
the grey aluminum wall of the train
vibrating
behind their kiss.

His upper lip stretched
taffy-like
before her lips released it,
their bodies swayed
as the train jolted,
and her lower lip retracted
from between his.

The kiss continued
for miles
beginning under city lights,
then further and further
through suburbs then fields

until a haggard woman,
child on knee
baby in stroller
barked, "Hey!
There are kids here!"

ruining it,
for the rest of us
wistful
and bitter
because we'd never been kissed
like that.

Summer 2000 Sestina

I'd never felt so transparent as when
you'd trace the blue tributaries running
under my skin, wondering if I was
the whitest white girl you'd ever seen. It
seemed perfect, waking up, you studying
my eyelashes, golden in the sunlight.

The open drapes billowed, filled with sunlight,
a day brimming with potential when
we'd drink juice at the window studying
all the brightly colored joggers running
around that lake so huge we'd pretend it
was the ocean, and in a way it was.

Otherwise, how ridiculous it was
to name regions after coasts, shores. Sunlight
heated the windowsill where we leaned. It
reminded us that time was short, the days when
we could be together swiftly running
out. We'd too soon be back to studying

at our separate schools—you, studying
your odd dichotomy—Art/CompSci was
your way of hedging bets. Running
from prudence was my style. I'd eat sunlight,
drink poetry, breathe novellas, and when
I'd had my fill, I'd leave you the rest. It

was this difference, I think, that ended it.
Me, studying you, and you studying
me. We never seemed to get it right when
we thought about what this difference was.
We should have treasured those days of sunlight,
our strolls in the park, when we kept running

commentary on the gazes running
up and down our bodies—if they knew it
just by looking at us. Your smile, sunlight
warm on my skin, my devout studying
of your long-limbed grace—my religion—was
the only thing on my mind those days when

our love was new—innocent as sunlight.
How foolish we were, studying it when
as with all new things, mistrust sent it running.

Rebuttal Evidence

Because I've been loving in my own way all along,
just today, on the drive home from work on that stretch of 12
that still slices through the cornfields, I was recalling Memorial Day
like it was last weekend and wondering what you're doing
in your new city, and when I got home to write you about it,
the message, ending like some job interview gone wrong
(*Take care of yourself and best of luck in your future*)
swam before me. I take that back. I won't be melodramatic.
The only words that have ever swum, the ink dissolving into snakes
before my eyes, I opened on February 4th 1998,
and read *terrible news   accident   killed* and knew that life
had irrevocably changed
despite the cheery promise of the pink envelope
and the WE'VE MOVED address label in the upper left hand corner.

If I can't love, as you say, then why do I sometimes pick up the phone
        or hear
the creak of a door and think *It's him?*
That's different, you might say,
and maybe you'd be right because the dead can't hurt us
and we certainly can't hurt them, so maybe they are easier to love,
at least for me. Maybe this is my abstract way of loving,
which I didn't ask for, but which seems to have always been my way—
that existential struggle between the self and other—
the way I never see where I end and begin in relation to the world,
which somehow always seems to puzzle or offend.

Once, when a little girl, about three years-old,
kept leaning into my face,
talking three year-old talk, and patting me with dimpled, chubby
hands, asking *Can I sit on your lap? Can I sit on your lap?*
I froze, not knowing how to ask her mother to take her away,
the cold sweat and blood pounding through my body
as I tried to catch my breath.
I love children, I tell friends, *as long as there's an ocean between us*

and it involves me sending them money
because doesn't it do more good to send $28 a month
to a child in a country with a per capita income of $236 USD
than to raise a child here where it costs $160,000 from birth
to age eighteen, not including college? This cost-benefit analysis
means one could raise 26 Cambodian children,
for the price of one American child.
This is my odd economics of emotion, but not any less
loving than the woman in the park pushing the toddler on the swings.

                          If I didn't love you, why did I write letters
to your Congressman to keep the black bears alive in your state,
or give up weekends working on a campaign so that you
could be safely black and bisexual in your new corner of the country?
Why would I bother to stop the aerial gunning of wolves in Alaska
unless I was saving them for us all? And can't you see
that we're all *all* of us? Maybe I'm afraid of that little girl because
          she's me.
In a few years she might accidentally let the vet take both dogs away
to new homes, not just the one that was chasing cattle,
and might still cry over him sometimes twenty years later
and wonder if he was happier, going with
Coffee to some old lady who wanted company on her farm;
then she might grow up to be loved but not love back
the way others do, instead inspiring a concerto
which is never played because the composer can't stand to think of her,
or being the reason a boy had to leave for North Carolina
because he couldn't bear to see her
even at the gas station in their town, or maybe she'll model
for a photographer ex-lover who will someday send her this email
that ends *Even if I've misinterpreted, I'd still rather*
not be in contact, so you won't hear from me again.

A Letter to Aya Ishibashi

Aya Ishibashi, how your name has stayed with me
though I never knew you—just another girl at the same college—
but the music of your name still floats through my mind at intervals I
    can't explain
the way songs from my childhood sprang back when I had to sing
to ward off bears while hiking Mt. Brown, tripping down the switch-
    backs.

Your name is in my language, too. It means "bird"
which makes me think of your hair, black, like a raven's wing,
and the way it undulated down your narrow back.
Something about the sound "Ay-ah" is lovely
in a hushed way like the herons I watched for every time I drove down
Lake-Cook Road. They stood so still against it all, the currents
of the water, the willows swaying in the breeze, a Chinese brush painting
amidst the urban sprawl, while we all raced to the expressway to race
even faster to somewhere else.

Aya means "colorful" in your language. Is that why you are an artist?
And married to a man whose last name is Black?
Perhaps only an artist would know it takes all the colors to make black—
    and—
Voila! You, teaching art, at the same school together, in California.
What if our fate is controlled by our names? I know, an easy argument
for me to make, whose name means "pretty," though this has inspired
    jabs
about my parents' keen sense of irony.

My ex-husband's name means "little and fair-haired"—which fit just as
    much,
but I couldn't put them so closely together—the Jewish and Irish, which
    sounded
like the beginning of some joke about someone entering a bar,
so I separated them with two other Hebrew names
and a hyphen for good measure

which a student called "a Shoah train with a 'Mick' caboose."
He offered to marry me to his cousins so I could Beers-Mendelssohn-Marx-
Markowitz on into eternity like those soap opera characters
or Zsa Zsa Gabor,
but I think I've been named quite enough
and sometimes winced at the cheery upbeat
on the end of a perfectly somber name.
Your laugh, I think I heard it once, fell through the air like silk,
and you looked like a dream, and your boyfriend thought
I was a good kid and talked to me.

Why It Almost Never Ends with Stripping

You start out doing it for the bucks—
more than you'd ever imagined,
enough, at first, to make up for the rest
of the shit that comes along with the job—
the groping despite the "No Touching" sign,
the bastards who bring in straight girls to con-

vince them they're bi, the girls nervous and con-
tinously fidgeting, while cash—
sweat-stained tens—shake in their hands, signaling
you over to dance while they imagine
themselves anywhere but there. "It's a job,"
you tell yourself, you'll just hold out the rest

of the summer. But you realize the rest
of the girls said the same thing, and they've con-
templated quitting for years, give blowjobs
in the back for fucking crazy money.
You don't want to be them but imagine
living the way they do, see them signing

five-figure checks on shopping sprees, signing
feature dancer contracts at clubs. You wrest
with the fact that girls who have the image
of putting out make ten times more. Buy con-
doms. Keep them on you just in case. The sugar's
pouring in—you're only giving handjobs.

You hear what you can make at outside jobs
doing bachelor parties, you're signing
on for three most weekends, making it
hand over fist, stripping at clubs the rest
of the week. The girl who dances as Con-
suela Cummings says she can imagine

you being "the next big thing. Imagine
your picture on boxes—Not just a job,
a career!" You read over the contract—
mark Xs for things you'll do, or not, sign
on the line—$5k if you check the rest—
anal, gangbang, scat bring in the greenbacks.

These days you don't read contracts, you just sign
to compete with the rest of the gravy-
starved girls who try to imagine it's just a job.

To CKC, Stillborn, April 22, 2006

Little flicker flame of a person, too fragile
to survive the world you were pushed out into—
I study charts of *20 weeks after conception*
24 weeks—and wonder where in that odd float
between miscarriage and *pre-term* you fell
and learn new terms—*Lanugo*—
the fine, downy hair covering a fetus,
new facts—that you must have weighed
between ten ounces and a pound
(the size of a three to five week old kitten)
but still picture a girl looking like your mother,
only smaller. Hair as fine and black as raven's
wings. Tiny eyes I see open from naps
when friends bring babies back from China,
cooing magical incantations to lure them to sleep,
mei-mei, bao, chan juan.
Your mother had such hopes for you,
wanted you to save her, needed to save herself
to save you but couldn't and fell back
into the life and the bottle and needle
we all try to save each other from,
your adopted aunts who have loved your mother
for the little girl in her
the one who comes back and is taken away
every few years when she remembers her brother
prying his way into her, giving her to friends
in exchange for marijuana, booze, all those things
that seem valuable when we are young,
but which is infinitely old
to you, who will always be twenty weeks
too young to be born
who will always be just out of reach
another untouchable girl on the periphery—
the one who gets to be safe.

Overview of the Carbon Cycle

I should have known when he rolled his eyes after I hushed
him so I could hear the news of Ginsberg's death

so many signs I should have seen

the photo of him with Reagan   a smiling Young Republican
complete with blue wool blazer

the day in the Art Institute when the boy-artist stopped
sketching to watch my languid admiration of lines and
colors and he   angry asked   why every *art freak in the
universe* noticed me   *I'm one of them* I murmured   and he
stepped back as if I'd confessed to having sex with a goat
Don't say that—don't ever say that again

We were light-years apart   political quizzes   personality
tests   as alike as kumquats and dump trucks   only our
bodies betrayed us to each other

on blankets in fields   in cars   the aseptic yuppie apart-
ment he kept me trapped in on breaks from school

but it took death to wrench us apart   for good

and someday if we rejoin our atoms reduced by chemical
change to the same humus
     will our carbon bases combine $12H_2O + 6CO_2 \rightarrow 6O_2 +$
$C_6H_{12}O_6 + 6H_2O$
to burst forth the head of the same daffodil? still serving
separate functions the sameness yet difference of   xylem
and phloem?

Rewind

Fridays Mrs. Wampler would give in
and leave the projector light on
as the film wound from one reel to the other.

At six, the world moving backward amazed us
more than the world moving forward,
though that amazed us, too.

Full blooms squeezed back into buds;
seedlings hid themselves underground,
but our favorite was our claymation version

of Beauty and the Beast. We would cheer as each
petal affixed itself to the thorny stem
and the beast grew stronger, clap as Beauty

no longer wept at his deathbed. And soon,
he was a prince again, too polite to ever
insult a crone. This taught us that beginnings

are always best, despite all they say about
Happily Ever After. If we could invent
the automatic rewind, bodies would expel

bullets that would rest eternally in chambers,
130,000 people would materialize
as the Enola Gay swallowed the bomb,

landmines would give legs and fingers
back to broken children.
Right now, teeming cancer cells

would be rebuilding blood and bone.

A Study in Weights and Measures

She punches ruthlessly—like the women at the gym
who've taken kickboxing,
but there's something different, so I ask who she's hitting,
and she says "Cancer," and I wish I knew how to fight
because when I first heard the word in relation to myself,
I thought *God, at last a rest*, and pictured a few months of time alone
to think and read and sleep in,
perhaps so long that I would feel ready to again take on the burden
of this world that has become so heavy in so short a time
that I don't know why people fight back to carry it even longer—

except there's still a lot I want, things that may seem silly.
Climb Mt. Brown (elevation 7,487 ft) though it's just a hill
to people who've climbed Everest or Kangto or Antofalla, because I'm
       ashamed
I made it only halfway, a testament to my lack of discipline—just like
my meager writings which I held next to my *Complete Works of Keats*,
who died only one year older than I was when I came back from my
       doctor.
This all seems panicked, looking back a year later,
but now, all tests negative, there's the bleeding
again, appointment three days away, and my head feels as light
as the balloon I let go in Mrs. Chamberlain's kindergarten class
with my name and address tied to the string
so that someone would write back to tell me how far it went—
maybe to Ohio or Kentucky, depending on the speed
and direction of the wind.

       And though the test seems so close, there's so much
blood I wonder if, like that balloon, I'll lose my grounding,
float away like that red speck—smaller, smaller, gone.

Surgery

Cold seeps
up   through the thin mat
        they've rolled me onto
settles   in my pelvic bones
        Second time
        under
the knife in four weeks
        First time
        to see   why the bleeding
hasn't stopped for months
        Second time
removing cells threatening
to turn into cancer
        Each time a microscopic
unsexing   more bits / more chunks / of me
        removed
Next time (if there is one)   I will
        float up
        listen in as they work   find out
if the small-talk jokes they make   as their faces
        become blurry are for them
        or for me
If I really look ten years younger
        than my chart says   If the reason
they are sparing my uterus   is so I can have
        a little girl with stoic grey eyes
gold sunflowers in their centers

Body Shop

I've promised parts to other men—
a right arm in exchange for attention,
a hand in marriage—
but I've decided to save you the good ones
and cut away the rest—
fifteen pounds of fat,
keeping just enough to stay
a woman.
Slice the pale blue moons
from under my eyes and leave you
just the crystal orbs,
unroot the tooth chipped on the roller coaster,
the ones with enamel fillings, give you the others like
pearls on a tray.
Pop out the cyst from my imperfect hand,
remove the right breast—
it has a birthmark and is smaller—
turn the rest of me inside out and
serve it up
all raspberry silk on a silver platter.

What Will We Do With You? This Bone Has Almost No Flesh Protecting It—

But I am like any porcelain doll, waiting to be destroyed
by a hammer. Brothers do these things
to incite the cries of their sisters. They think
This is power. Someday they will learn that power
is smiling gleefully up at the anvil. Where I am from,
everyone looks like a corpse. We are ivory
and blue-veined until cooled at 0° for 28–32 minutes.
Then we begin to color up—cheeks become pink,
eyes, a teary blue, lips, a red slash,
sometimes painted crooked by a drunken artist.
Because, as Linus Torvalds said, "there is nothing to
do at home but drink." Where I want to take you
the mountain passes are cleared in July—
until it snows at the end of August and some years
Hidden Lake is always under snow, but I
will climb until I find it. Though you seem
to be made of sand and fashioned for warmth,
I will lock you in a cabinet—porcelain dolls are
dangerous like this sometimes. You and I are not
so different, the same color when the sun shines
through the khaki sheets. But this sun is too much.
Even the sheets can't stop it—It is scarier than
the hammer. This sun, even in the morning,
in February, is going to obliterate us all.

Wind Advisory

That year I loved you most, it seemed
like it was windy all the time.
That year I loved you most,
windows rattled, sixty mile per hour gales
keened over every surface,
as we took refuge in our bed, slept so much
we couldn't fight.
The year I loved you most was
five years ago
and it seems safe to love you again.

Last night's storm reminded me
how small I used to feel
cradled against you
and how big the world seems even now.

And how I still love you
enough to want to join you
under the autumn leaf-covered ground
of Oak Hill Cemetery,
small and insignificant as if we were still
hiding under covers.

In a Top Drawer

Unaware that touching cottontail rabbits
gives them pneumonia, out of the best
of intentions, we tried to save them.

My mother bought babydoll bottles; we fed them
milk replacement, changed the hot water bottle hourly
so they wouldn't miss their mother's warmth.

Eight in all, we named them. But one by one
they perished, leaving tiny graves in the back yard.
And I invented my odd religion,

pretending they had been reincarnated
in my bean bag rabbit—and talked to him
every night, murmuring their names.

The first year after you were gone
I saw you everywhere. Every blond man
was you. In the grocery. Behind the cello

at the orchestra—Right now, there's
a mannequin of you sporting a suit
and tie in a nearby suburb.

Things haven't changed much between
the six year-old girl tending rabbits
and me. Your mother's letter rests

in a top drawer next to a report card
where Mrs. Brown wrote in the comments section
How are your rabbits?

Cicadas

Where will we be the next time
they emerge, in 17 years,
when brood X nymphs first wriggle their way
out of exit holes, climb the trunks of oaks and maples,
sun themselves on viburnum,
pale and helpless, before their wings dry
and darken
so they can fly safely to trees to mate, lay eggs,
and die?
I'm not sure I have a concept of 17 years.
I remember Ronald Reagan was President,
I was jealous of my friend Lindsey because
she had a Debbie Gibson hat.
The Princess Bride came out, and is still
my favorite movie.
Seventeen years in the future seems daunting.
The boys at the little league field behind my house
will be men, the neighbors' dog will be dead
and the tree in my backyard
will no longer be mine.
I could be living anywhere—
not one to put down roots, I can't even guess.
Just yesterday, I realized, looking out your window,
that in less than two months
new trees will greet me from another window.
No longer the canopy of hardwoods,
but lush, tropical greens year-round
1,300 miles away from you.
And though we've talked about this,
I wonder what you're thinking,
what you would like to be doing
with the seventeen years that this year's
nymphs will spend underground,
burrowing, living on the roots of all those trees.

My Love, A Partial Explanation

You ask what was different this time,
and I answer that it was the combination of rocks and water
and make some obscene joke about the sexual escapades
which would have ensued had we been in Maine or Oregon,

but this is because I don't know how to tell you about your eyes,
which you think are brown, but which I know are gold-flecked
in different lights, and the way they smiled
when we talked our odd talk about relationships
and the stars; not really astrology,
more astrodynamics and Eagles' lyrics with a bit
of quantum theory thrown in for good measure,

and I don't know what you see in me,
but I knew you were closer to the truth than anyone else
when you said that my body reminded you
of South Dakota, because I always knew I was a plains
state—only the colors of sand and wheat and
eyes as grey as storm clouds, which used to anger my mother
because she thought if only I'd had more color,
I could be beautiful—

                        The other day when we watched the geese,
and you said, wistfully, *Soon there will be goslings,*
I didn't mean to be a bitch and say *Poor, monogamous bastards,*
but sometimes life is so structured, and I'm always
on the outside, never quite able to figure out the rules
that everyone seems to take for granted.

I've been told that loving me is like loving a guard dog,
you're never sure if it's love, or if you're just grateful
that you're the one thing it won't kill;
and I don't know how to stop this,

it just seems to be my way. The way that giraffes
are my favorite animal, not only because they're so gentle,
but because a mother giraffe can decapitate a lion
with a single kick if it threatens her calf.

Flashback

The ceiling postered, laundry-strewn room takes us back
fifteen years. Early 80s punk reminds us of parents
we still don't speak to—because once an outsider,
always an outsider—and we arrange garage sale treasures
he's collected this week. Tiny prosperity Buddahs and
Harry Potter at a podium line a shelf, when I reach for
metal shine, and at once I am four and bouncing
on the black cloth seat of the 1972 Nova, looking back
through the dust wake our car makes that dry, Indiana summer.
I ask where we are going, but Mom is driving through
soybeans, cornfields, and tears. The compass tells something,
but what? That silver snow globe without glitter bobs
on the windshield—South—and—West—and—South.
Baby sister sucks on a bottle, and as we drive through hotter
and hotter, Mom makes me drink from it " 'Cause
we're not stopping until we're far enough away."
I am four and do not understand "far enough" because
under my feet is a clothesbasket, piled with the toys
she shrieked for us to gather as she taped a note
to the dust-gray screen of the TV, packed a diaper bag,
a suitcase. When you are four, you don't realize
that a road can go on forever, take you from forest
to wheat field to desert, that there are worlds you
have never known. Worlds where the dull sound
of your mother's body hitting a wall, a door, the baby's
changing table are as alien as saying *I love you.*

Taking Back the Bra Drawer

I started by giving away, slowly, the left side—
first the top of the dresser, where there was
always a pile of his clothes—workman's pants,
long sleeved tie dyes. There is still a handcrafted belt,
heavy with an eagle buckle. Then I tucked
his laundry—clean—into the bra drawer.
Donated the impulse buys to the Salvation Army
to make room for his khaki cargo shorts,
grey thermal bottoms. The solid heaviness
of a man crowded out the florals and polka dots.
His scent—patchouli and work—is worn into
the flannel bedding I bought to keep us through winter.
A hockey puck of mint snuff rests on the carpet
next to the bed. He is everywhere—his
tape measurer keeps the kitchen counter from
escaping. And yet—after a normal argument—
when I suggested he stay at his place tonight—
and he decided to stay there for all nights—
I want him here to the degree
of absenting myself. I will be any woman—
one who hasn't slept with other women, or
who hasn't been married before—one who will
sew by hand until she is needle-pricked dry.
I don't want him to be another man—
another box of leftover belongings in a closet
waiting to be picked up,
another man whose name I use to describe
a period in my life,
another man whose jewelry rests in a hidden
drawer, worn only as an accessory to
regret. Another man whose children
will not giggle when I balloon sky blue
cotton sheets against the ceiling.

Mother

Nights, after you pulled out your pink gown
edged with mink,
beaming that someday it would be mine

I would whimper myself to sleep,
too young to fathom your gift
for cruelty.

You laughed and
nicknamed me Gandhi
the time I tried to save the gnat

struggling in a water droplet
leftover from my toothbrushing
and I cried, knowing I was responsible.

You stopped me from unwrapping
the plastic lining

on the lampshade
to save the trapped moth,

but I am no Gandhi.

Even then, when I read histories
of our people,
I pictured Nazis

making lampshades
of your stretched hide,

stuffing mattresses
with your chestnut hair,

and dreamed a chorus of laughing animals.

Moonlight Sestina

Something in me changed that night there with you,
surrounded by snow, wading through moonlight,
lost in a dreamland too pure to be real,
inebriated with your charm, your touch,
praying it wasn't infatuation,
needing it to be more than that for once.

We labeled it a lapse that happened once—
why build dreams together of me and you?
Safer to call it infatuation—
blame it on Christmas lights, stars, and moonlight,
deny the unearthly glow of our touch—
than to take a chance at something much more real

because magic should never transcend "real."
It's much more romantic to have a "once"
than to let what we shared cool to the touch
like countless others before me and you
who didn't have sense to blame the moonlight
for drowning them in infatuation.

I don't accede to *infatuation*
as the verdict; I think it could be real—
just inspired by Vermont snow in moonlight
(though we decided it was just a "once")
and I'll not think that way again of you
and promise not to dream about your touch

though now I recoil from another's touch
and am ill from lack of "infatuation,"
certain the only antidote is you.
I wish we'd had the nerve to make it real,
to say without regret those words which once
uttered, we retracted from the moonlight

because what kind of witness is moonlight
that we should care that it saw my hand touch
your cheek for a fleeting second, just once,
and linger, held fast by infatuation,
wanting to be that snowflake?—something real
and pure and innocent and close to you.

Now, when I see moonlight, I think of you,
wondering if our "once" could have been real
or my wits just "touched" by infatuation?

Branching

Now that I've learned that the almond and peach
are members of the same family, it all makes sense.
Since childhood, I'd wondered how an almond had managed to imbed
itself in the middle of all that fleshy stuff without ever wounding
the human-esque skin and making all the juice dribble
out the side. And now that I've been schooled and over-schooled,
this same train of thought makes me think that perhaps
Derrida was right—that the center is not the center,
but is perhaps the center of something else
whether we are speaking of time, language, the universe—
peaches, or almonds.
And I'm sad to have learned that the tasty part
of a fruit is its mesocarp, which makes me not especially like peaches
though before I knew this, they were my favorite fruit.

It's this link between almond and peach that gives me hope
that someday I'll become something else
if I don't manage to become what I've aimed for,
like the unsold bagels at the coffee shop across from the college
that are made into bagel chips at the end of the week
and given away free with each order of spinach dip.
I'm certain this isn't at all what those bagels
in all their multitudinous types dreamed of—
perhaps the cheddar-jalapeño in the glassed-in case,
resting between the poppy seed and honey-wheat-
rolled-in-whole-grain-oats, once thought, that
as a more exotic bread, it would be taken home
in a variety pack, or sliced and toasted in-store,
then bagged and eaten at a desk, or
lazily enjoyed with a gourmet coffee
right there in the shop while its devourer
lingered over the paper

but this is a problem I've always had,
assigning human thought to all objects,
and my main criticism of that is this—
I've seen little evidence of humans thinking
at all. Or why, that time
when my coupon read *Three 20 ounce*
boxes for $5 and there were no 20 ounce boxes left,
when I took four 15 ounce boxes, did the cashier say
I couldn't do that and then she called a manager
who explained to her that 3 times 20 is the same
as 4 times 15, or how about
the guy I car-pooled with to teach
at the all-Black school, who said one day
I wouldn't care if that entire place blew up
but I didn't know what to say,
so I stared out the window at the blur of sky
and passing trees,
not accomplishing much more
than those bagels behind the glass,
waiting, waiting, for someone to notice me
to make me something more.

The Calypso Diaries

I.

I did not let him go because Zeus told me to,
nor because I had grown weary
of his love.
It's just that sometimes a girl's got to know
that a man is happier with a woman than with
a goddess, even a minor one.
If you promise him immortality on an island,
it just means you'll be walking the same beach,
century in and century out;
with Penelope, he'll have another thirty, forty years
tops. They'll watch Telemachus grow
into a man and laugh at the folly of all those suitors,
while I sit here, enjoying sunset
after sunset
after sunset
and all the quiet of the world.

II.

Sometimes you let him go because it is more cruel
than keeping him.
Sometimes you let him go because freedom
is the opposite of love.
Sometimes you let him go because freedom
is the only love.
Sometimes you let him go because there is only
one Penelope.
Sometimes you let him go because there is only one Calypso
and you know that he will think of her more often
from across the sea.

III.

Watching the raft disappear into the horizon
is bittersweet
because you wish him favorable winds
and send him with enough provisions
to know he'll look back on you kindly,
but you get to wondering if your heart was too big,
why you smoked and dried your fattest sow
and cross-cut your tallest cedars for the raft

to take him back to Ithaca
and Penelope
her pale arms
their oaken bed.

IV.

It's the same double-standard, always;
a god can sleep with as many
mortals as he wants
but a goddess takes a man as a lover
and Zeus must intervene.
I decried Zeus for his indiscretions
with Leda and Europa,
but, alas, he's Zeus, and there's no reasoning.
When I uttered Leda's name, I faltered,
because she's the reason for Helen
and this insipid war.
At the crack in my voice, Zeus
chuckled—I knew my case was lost
but tried every trick possible,
Odysseus isn't really a mortal—
he's almost a god, or why would Athena,
your daughter, from your own head sprung,

so adore him? Or
Odysseus is less than a mortal—
it was pity. He washed up on my shore,
more a half-drowned kitten than a man—
can I keep him?
But none of these worked.
Zeus, who must have Hera and Leda
and Europa and many others
can't understand the curse
of being alone
and immortal
in paradise.

V.

Sometimes there are centuries between shipwrecks
and I picture ravaged vessels,
their crews scattered
on other islands
with Circe and Nausikaa,
and other goddesses I have never heard of
while I watch the sky pinken
and grey,
pinken and grey.
I scratch names of long-dead men
in the sand
with my palm frond
and watch the surf
erase the beach
the way time restores my mind
to peace,
the way Odysseus' back was healed from
Circe's fingernail welts by the time
he washed ashore.

Belonging

My cat gets used to her collar
the way I got used to my wedding ring.
I still fidgeted with it
five years in. It was the first thing
I took off when I got home.
I try to explain to her that it's for
protection. So that if she gets lost
someone who finds her
will know that she belongs
to someone,
and I wonder if this is what he thought
when he gave me this ring.

Fifteen years ago, in a Sunday school class,
we were asked *If you could have a dinner party
with any three people dead or alive,
who you would pick?*
I couldn't think of any choices
except for my cat.
Everyone laughed. But she's still here.

Now we're going away. Just me and her,
starting over. She's been with me
through five boyfriends, four girlfriends,
one marriage. When we drive South
she'll be wearing her lavender collar.
I'll be the one with bare hands.

Outdoor Cafe, Lake Mary, FL

Today, where the water saw only sky
it shone back blue,
but at the edges where it reflected trees and earth
it was the color of your eyes.
It seems right that something as simple as a pond
can hold us both.
A female blackbird landed at my table
and I didn't know her
until another diner introduced us.
Similar to the male only in shape
and not deserving of the name *blackbird*
because of her paprika feathers,
I pitied her and fed her my heart in bits of bread.
The wind pushed the reeds in the slow rhythm
of your heart—that too-slow steadiness
that uneases us because it seems just moments away
from stopping like the heart of your father this summer—
your biggest fear, other than loneliness.
These come together in the night when we lie
in the quiet and you say *This is how
I don't want to wake up someday.*
I listen, as I do every night, for the peaceful affliction
of slower, slower, none, and dream of us sinking
into the earth around us,
the couch disintegrating, our building falling
into ruin, as we become embedded like a sliver
in a palm. So small and insignificant, the world
would never notice.

Omens

The bathroom clock in the dying man's house
is stopped at thirteen 'til two. I search for
signs that are less ominous. I sigh,
glad to remember that a stopped clock's right
twice a day, it's the ones we push ahead
that are never so. I shrug off my dread,
wash it down the sink. Then head out
again to pull the weeds from the borders
of the trees. The weeds are as certain as death.
I work to the rhythm of my breath,
try to take in great draughts of sunlight
as I cut through the immense tightness
of the roots—the roots, hanging on for life—
and imagine myself the dying man's wife.

Return

When the clouds come in over the lake, eggplant dark,
and the ice fishers are trudging in for the day,
I watch the vermilion opening of sun in clouds
and slip into a time when women wore indigo-dyed smocks
and wielded the hips, thighs, breasts of goddesses
as their religion. Every woman knows
how to be Circe or Medea until it's trained out of her
and she becomes Penelope or Portia,
waiting away her days or ending them
choking on coals. Maybe the way to the next world
lies somewhere beneath the ice, and all I've got to do
to find it is steal one of the ice fisher's saws
and make my circle—ignore the pangs and stabs
of ice between my ribs, in my lungs—and swim further,
deeper than any submersible has ever been,
brushing away the warnings of Celsius and Fahrenheit
and Kelvin, any advice of modern medicine.
Because I know this is my lake
and it won't hurt me
despite what scientists, philosophers, other observers might
think, because sometime when myth was real
I lived there, and now I need to go back, feel my legs merge
        again into fins
and swim through time. Have tea with the Lady of the Lake,
laugh with the Sirens at their stories, shudder at tales of
strange men cutting holes to the realm above.

Weekend Rain Ghazal

Because I have you this weekend, I should thank the endless
    Portland rain.
The summer I was eleven, men drove bullets into their heads
    for lack of rain.

Too often, loving someone requires not just a heart and a body
    but a wallet.
My English teacher told me not to marry a farmer; my whole
    life would depend on rain.

I sit in a Main Street bar and order a beer the darkness of your
    eyes.
Their Alaskan Amber is the color of my hair; my eyes are
    clouds filled with rain.

You lock your bike to a two-hour-parking sign, wave through
    the window of the bar.
Being together in public is unnerving. We've been hiding
    ourselves away, like birds, from rain.

In the quiet of flannel sheets, a clicking heater, we've been
    the entire world.
The radiator in the old house sounds like a tin roof being
    worked over by rain.

Surgery scars can make a man look like a baseball, a warrior,
    a map.
When I was eight, I sewed split seams of stuffed toys,
    whispered, "Dr. Beers to surgery."

I Give You Words

Because the body is so ephemeral and corrupt,
what is beautiful today may not be so ten years hence,
I give you words.
Because my thoughts are strange and dreamlike
and not to be trusted to icon or art,
I put them into words for you.
Words that may or may not be said
from one of us to the other or from one of us
to another after we have parted—these words
of memories made or imagined,
of beaches walked or not,
of fruit trees planted or not,
and then harvested or not.
The very potential of all of this—
like a speck of sand the temperature of the sun
slowly baking the earth.
Sometimes there are no words,
and I am tempted to make up new ones,
but what could new words do that others
in their lives of thousands of years could not accomplish?
The way that physicists have made up the *white* hole,
which is not its own thing, but merely the antithesis
of the *black* hole—the way *antithesis* was made up, too.
So I try to use old words, inherited from generation
after generation, and try to make them say new things
as if there was never love before us
on this earth, as if every day we're not drinking
and breathing the molecules of long-dead lovers
who thought they, too, had invented love,
who felt these same tensions and betrayals
and tried to use old words to describe these hopes
and glories of the flesh and mind, and failed
as I have, to say the thing anew.

Because You Are In It

I am in love with the world because you are in it.
I am in love with your city, and all its streets and alleyways.
The black cat sitting near the dumpster at the bar.
The girl at the coffee shop—a sort of urban Madonna
with short dyed-red hair, and tattoos. A baby nearly as big
as she is rides her hip between tables. When she bends over
to put him down, the five-pointed star on her lower back
rises from a denim sea.
I am in love with her awkward beauty—
her too-big nose, her overbite.
I want to live in the hipbone that juts from
the waistband of her jeans.
I am in love with the lake and the hum
of the trawlers
and the iridescent wake of oil they leave behind.
With the fine-legged water bugs that oar
their way across its surface.
I love the last drops of wine in the glass
next to the bed, because they have touched others
that touched your lips
and the sun shines claret
through them—the same sun that shone
through my eyes this morning
when you woke next to me.

Tonight in this hotel room's mirrored wall ...

> "Things are beautiful if you love them."
> —JEAN ANOUILH

Tonight in this hotel room's mirrored wall,
we strip each other's bodies of wet clothes.
We are Adam and Eve, after the fall.

I trace ink, scars, wholly enthralled,
kiss the incisions that have kept you close.
Tonight in this hotel room's mirrored wall

the branches of your arms make me small.
We seem mismatched, trapped, in an unnatural pose.
We are Adam and Eve, after the fall.

We name imperfection the best beauty of all—
my striped thighs, your once-opened chest, broken nose—
tonight in this hotel room's mirrored wall.

Something in us answered a primal call,
locking ourselves indoors while the storm blows,
we are Adam and Eve, after the fall.

Unmarked beauty is not beauty to all;
pity and love from these scars arose.
Tonight in this hotel room's mirrored wall
we are Adam and Eve, after the fall.

How Time Betrays Us

Right now, I am 27 in human years.
My cat is 83.

My sexual peak will occur in approximately 8 years.
My lover's was 19 years ago.

According to a 2002 study, my fertility is already declining.
I still believe beer, cheesecake, and chocolate are the main
food groups.

Every day around the world, 120 million people make love.
Today is not my day.

In the time it will take you to read this,
somewhere, in America, a woman was raped.

171,233 animals were slaughtered for human consumption.
32 children worldwide died of starvation.

I may have already died, but you are reading this,
thinking I am 27 and very much in love.

Printed in the United States
136181LV00001B/6/P